T0165271

Take Control of Your Life

Pauline Parsons

authorHOUSE®

AuthorHouse™
1663 Liberty Drive
Bloomington, IN 47403
www.authorhouse.com
Phone: 1-800-839-8640

First published by AuthorHouse 4/28/2011

ISBN: 978-1-4567-2843-4 (e)
ISBN: 978-1-4567-2845-8 (sc)

Library of Congress Control Number: 2011900842

Printed in the United States of America

Foreword

These days more than ever before, it seems as if many of us do not have control over the things that are happening in our lives. It may be that you have lost your job due to the economic downturn or you have just found out that you have lung cancer. In both cases, this is a devastating experience. While in life we have to deal with circumstances beyond our control, there are things that we can do to help us cope when bad things happen. It may be that we have no savings to fall back on when we lose a job or have to leave the work force due to a medical condition and have no short-term disability insurance to get us through financially or that we smoke cigarettes even though we know how harmful cigarette smoking is to our health. This book is about money matters and health matters and what consequences they may have in our lives past, present and future. Knowledge is power. If people have knowledge about the matters of money and in particular health, they are able to make better choices for themselves. I wrote this book to make people more aware of the things they can do to have more control in their lives. We must take control of the things in which we can and do it now. There is no time to waste! This book is divided into two segments making it a quick and easy reference guide.

SEGMENT I

MONEY MATTERS

Chapter 1
Saving in 2011 and Beyond

The days of wastefulness are gone and thrifty is in. Yes, you read that correctly, thriftiness is now in vogue whether you are rich or poor. At almost every income bracket, Americans are changing their buying habits and deciding they can live without certain things. American shoppers are now viewing cheaper as the better route to go. No longer is the SUV a must have and the small car is the vehicle of choice, store brands are being purchased over the fancy labels and shoppers in general prefer to shop the discount stores over the full service stores. Americans are choosing to stretch their dollars. Simply put, paychecks are not stretching as far as they used to due to high energy, food and medical costs; so, we are doing whatever is necessary to make ends meet. Saving is now a necessity.

One of the purposes of this book is to make you more aware of the many ways you can save money in this economic climate, especially if you would like to continue doing the fun things you have always enjoyed doing such as traveling, fine dining on those special occasions or even enjoying early retirement. And so you ask, how can I save money today?

A. Save, Save, Save:

1. If you smoke, you need to quit **NOW**. I know that smoking is one of the most difficult habits to quit, but if you want to badly enough, you will. One must put mind over matter. In Boston where I live, one can pay as much as $8.55 for a pack of cigarettes. The price of a pack of cigarettes keeps going up mostly due to taxes being added to the price. This tax tactic is being used as a deterrent to smoking. In New York City, Mayor Bloomberg has drastically increased the sales tax on a package of cigarettes. The price of a pack of cigarettes in New York City including tax is about $12.00. If you smoke a pack a day, the cost is $84.00/week, $336.00/month and $4,032.00/year. If you live in New York City and you smoke, you need to give this some serious thought. If you quit smoking, over a period of 25 years, you could have saved over **$100,000** just in the savings of the cost of the cigarettes. This does not even take into consideration any additional savings in medical expenses you may incur as a result of continuing to smoke cigarettes. The average price of a pack of cigarettes including tax in the United States is $5.00. If you smoke a pack a day, the cost is $35.00/week, $150.00/month and $1,800.00/year. Think about it, that could be two or three house payments a year or a nice vacation for you and your family or you might choose to invest the money you are saving. Let me give you an example. If you are forty years old and you make the decision to quit smoking cigarettes and put the money previously used to buy cigarettes into a 401K Plan earning 9% per year, you would have $250,000 by the age of 70. If the money reason is not enough to make you quit the

smoking habit, in a later chapter I will be discussing the medical costs associated with smoking and the possibility of a shortened life span.

2. If you carry balances on credit cards, pay the balances off as soon as possible. If you can only pay the minimum each month, then so be it, but discontinue usage of the credit card. Either cut up the credit card so you will not be able to use it any longer or hide it. Whatever you have to do, **STOP** using the credit card **NOW**. If you pay only the minimum each month, you are the loser and the bank or credit card company is the winner. Let me give you an example, if you have a balance of $7,000 on a credit card with an annual percentage rate of 8.24% and you pay only the minimum payment each month (approximately $117.00 on a $7,000.00 balance), it will take you 24 years to pay off the balance and you will have paid a total of $11,610.39. Of course this is without any late fees added on and no additional purchases made with the credit card. Now, if you paid more than the minimum payment, let's say $220.00 per month, it would take you 36 months to pay off the balance and you would have paid $7,970.76 in total which is a savings of $3,640.00! Think what you could do with $3,640.00. Wouldn't you rather have your hard earned money than give it to the bank? The amount of money banks make from the balances carried on credit cards is astronomical! All of us have heard and read, especially lately the amount of money banks made in the first quarter of 2010 alone. I will discuss credit cards in more depth in the next chapter.

3. Make Starbucks coffee a treat not an every day drink.

You will be surprised by the amount of money you will save by cutting back on the consumption of Starbucks coffee. I am not against Starbucks coffee; I like the Mocha Latte very much, but I have decided to make it a treat and not an every day pleasure. If it has to be Starbucks, buy a bag of Starbucks coffee and brew it at home. You will have your Starbucks and save money too.

4. Take lunches to work. It is much cheaper to brown bag it as opposed to dining out every day and it can be healthier as well, especially when you include fresh fruit and bottled water. Also, reuse the lunch bag, save a tree! Just to give you an example, if you saved $6.00/day x 5 days=$30.00/week. If you saved this amount for 10 years at 6% interest, you would have $19,592.00. Think about it, you would have saved almost $20,000.00!

5. Make going out for an ice cream cone a treat. Buy the ice cream and ice cream cones and make your own at home. If you have several children, this can be a big saving to you.

6. Buy snack foods in bulk and take to your office. Buy from the vending machine as a last resort.

7. Don't waste paper towels, wipe your hands with a hand towel.

8. Re-use plastic shopping bags as trash bag liners for the bathroom wastebasket.

9. If you have a green thumb, plant a vegetable garden

and/or flower garden. If you are having a dinner party, decorate the dinner table with fresh flowers from your flower garden.

SAVING TIP: At the average price of $5.00 for a pack of cigarettes, by quitting the pack a day smoking habit = a savings of $150.00/month and $1,800.00/year.

B. Conserve Gasoline:

1. Do all of your errands in one trip.

2. Carpool whenever possible.

3. Don't travel over 65 mph as it uses more gas.

4. Call the store first before making the trip to ensure that they are open and/or have the item you want.

5. Keep the engine tuned.

6. Keep the tires properly inflated.

7. Start slowly at green lights.

8. Slow down as you are approaching a red light as opposed to hard braking it when you get to the light.

9. Drive at a steady pace and use cruise control.

10. Lighten the load, remove unnecessary items from the trunk of the car.

11. Sell the SUV, buy a vehicle that gives you better gas mileage.

12. Take mass transportation whenever available.

13. Walk or ride your bike to work. It saves gas and helps the environment not to mention how good the exercise is for you.

14. Buy birthday cards one to two months in advance; this will eliminate unnecessary trips to the store.

15. Be a planner, make one trip to the grocery store each week as opposed to two or three.

16. When out running your errands, take the shortest route - no backtracking - saves time and gas.

17. Don't feel like you have to park right in front of the store, park a short distance away as this will save gas and give you some exercise.

SAVING TIP: Saving 8 gallons of gas each month at $3.00/gallon =$24.00/month and $288.00/year.

C. Conserve Electricity:

1. Turn off the lights when not needed.

2. Replace regular light bulbs with fluorescent bulbs.

3. In the winter months, lower the thermostat - put on a sweater.

4. Raise the setting on the air conditioner, use ceiling fans and keep blinds closed during the hot summer days.

5. If away from home for the day, turn off the hot water heater.

6. Unplug the television when not in use as a television draws current even when it is off.

7. Add nightlights to bathrooms and hallways.

8. Run the dishwasher at off-peak hours and run only when full.

9. Run the washing machine only with a full load of laundry, this saves energy and water.

10. When drying clothes in the dryer, do not dry completely rather finish drying clothes on an indoor drying rack.

11. Wash clothes in cold water.

12. When baking, bake 2 or 3 entrees at the same time,

freeze the extra or heat up for dinner the next night. This is a great time and energy saver.

SAVING TIP: Lower the thermostat and put on a sweater = $20.00/month and $240.00/year.

D. Saving Energy in the Home:

1. Replace old windows with new thermopane windows.

2. To help lower the heating bill, insulate the attic.

3. Install skylights and let the sun shine in. This not only gives more light to the room but helps to heat the room(s) especially during the winter months.

SAVING TIP: Replace old windows with new thermopane windows =$50.00/month and $600.00/year.

E. Saving at the Grocery Store:

1. Check the supermarket flyers for weekly specials to look for at the store. Be a comparison shopper; glance over the weekly sales and see what stores have the best prices and save by buying items on sale. If the item is nonperishable, buy at least two of the item while on sale and you are all set until the item goes on sale again.

2. Plan your meals around the items on sale each week. For example, if the poultry or beef is on sale, buy extra and put in the freezer.

3. Another way to save is to buy large family packs whether on sale or not as the larger sizes are usually cheaper per pound and split the cost with family members.

4. It pays to shop early at the supermarket as the meat department will offer $ off certain packages of meats that are close to their last sell date.

5. Be aware that many food items are sold at discount stores such as Dollar Tree and Family Dollar and they usually cost less than the grocery store.

6. Stick to a shopping list and your grocery budget. Most importantly, do not go shopping when you are hungry as you will buy everything in sight!!

7. Buy the store brands which are cheaper then the name brands and many times one cannot tell the difference but

there is a major difference in the price where as the name brand can cost as much as 25-30% more.

SAVING TIP: Buying sale items = $50.00/month and $600.00/year.

F. Coupons:

Coupons are back in fashion. Years ago, many people felt they could not be bothered with coupons; it just wasn't worth the time or the energy. This is no longer the case. The general feeling years ago was that it took time to look online for coupons or sort through coupon booklets and cut out coupons. Consumers are now finding that it is actually worth taking the time to collect and use coupons. The average saving per coupon is $1.44. If it takes one minute to clip and use a coupon, then your hourly rate would be $86.40 and that is tax-free. Not bad when you consider that the average wage for the American worker is approximately $20.00/hour. With that being said, it is hard to believe that 99% of all coupons today are thrown away unused. In comparison to a few years ago, coupons are making a big comeback. There were 3.3 billion coupons redeemed in 2009, a 27% increase from 2008 per CNN on January 29, 2010. The surge in coupon usage began in October of 2008. Some people have the coupon usage down to a science saving as much as 50% off of their weekly grocery bills. If you have never used coupons before, it behooves you to begin today!

SAVING TIP: Coupon usage = $100.00/month and $1,200.00/year.

G. Dining Out:

1. Dine out for breakfast or lunch not dinner as breakfast and lunch are usually the less expensive meals.

2. Eat at fast food restaurants and eat healthy as many of the fast food restaurants offer salads.

3. Use coupons whenever possible for dollars off of your meal. Consider purchasing an Entertainment Book if you dine out often.

4. Pay a visit to the grocery store and prepare the meal yourself as opposed to dining in a restaurant. Think of the money you will save in tipping alone. Preparing the food yourself is a money saver over buying frozen dinners as well.

5. Eating lunch out every day really gets expensive quickly; my advice is to limit the dining out to once a week.

SAVING TIP: Eating dinner out once a month vs. once a week for a party of two @ $50.00 (includes tip) = $150.00/month and $1,800.00/year.

H. Entertainment at Home:

1. Plan a barbeque and invite the family and friends over.

2. Rent a movie and make popcorn at home.

3. Invite friends over for a special TV program and serve coffee and dessert.

4. Swap dinner night - it's a great way to get together with friends at each other's homes on a weekly or monthly basis.

SAVING TIP: Renting a movie and having popcorn at home for a family of four = $40.00/month and $480.00/year.

I. Exercise:

1. Don't pay to join a gym. Walking is the best exercise there is and it's free! If you have space in your home, set up an exercise room with a stationary bike.

2. Don't join a Diet Program, walking and eating smaller portions will help you lose the weight you desire. Eat lots of fruits and vegetables.

3. Remember the fountain of youth is fitness and eating well.

4. Join a Wellness Program if offered by your employer. Wellness Programs aim to improve employee well-being with physicals, fitness guidance or other incentives to ward off future medical bills. Companies who offer wellness programs have found that sick days by their employees have decreased.

SAVING TIP: Walking on your own vs. joining a Health Club = $50.00/month and $600.00/year.

J. High-End Shopping for less:

1. Shop the outlet stores. Plan a trip to the nearest Outlet Mall and find those bargains. Most stores feature sales over the holidays which add up to additional savings for you.

2. If shopping in a Home Furnishing Store such as Polo-Ralph Lauren, be certain to check out the discontinued items section and you will find fantastic bargains.

3. If you are into Designer Clothing but don't want to pay the high prices, shop high-end consignment shops. Consignment Shops also carry fine leather goods so check them out as well. If you live in the Boston area as I do and want to check out a great consignment shop, I highly recommend The Second Time Around Clothing, 176 Newbury Street, Boston, MA. The telephone number is 617.247.3504.

SAVING TIP: Purchase a couple of Chanel Suits for $800.00 each at a Consignment Shop vs. a high-end retailer; a Savings of $2,000.00 each times 2 = $4,000.00/year.

K. Fun in the Sun:

1. If you reside only one or two hours from the ocean, pack a picnic lunch and drive there for the day. Don't pay to stay at an expensive hotel overnight unless it is a special occasion. Look at it this way, where else can you have such a beautiful view while dining on a picnic lunch. And, you can walk the beach after lunch.

2. Don't forget to take plenty of bottled waters, buying them cost far too much at local stores. For example, buying Poland Spring water (24 pack) for $3.99 on sale equates to only 16.6 cents/bottle.

SAVING TIP: Buying the Poland Spring Water (24 pack) on sale for $3.99 =16.6 cents each vs. $1.00 per bottle in the local store (24 bottles) would be $24.00 = a Savings of $20.01/month and $240.12/year.

Total Savings in 1 month = $654.01 and Total Savings in 1 year = $11,848.12. Imagine what you could do with **$10,000 plus!!!** If you have credit card debt of this amount or less, you could pay it off in full in one year.

Chapter 2
Credit Cards

We are inundated these days with the negative associated with using credit cards. There is nothing wrong with using credit cards providing you pay the balance in full when you receive the bill or at least pay the balance off within a few months. The problem arises when you max out one or more credit cards and have difficulty paying the minimum amount due each month. When you take into consideration the high interest rate you are paying when you don't pay the balance off in full each month, you can see that this is not a pretty picture. If it takes you several months or years to pay the credit card balance in full, you most likely have forgotten what you bought with the credit card in the first place. And as if this isn't bad enough, while you are paying off these old debts, you may find that it is necessary for you and/or your family to go without new clothes or shoes because there is no money in the budget for these things.

If you are deep in credit card debt, my advice is this regarding credit cards, **don't** use them! If you find you cannot stop using them, take the credit card(s) out of your wallet and hide them or better yet, cut them up so that you can no longer use them. Get yourself in the habit of paying by cash or debit card only. Paying with cash or your debit card puts you in more control of your finances which ultimately gives you more control of your life overall. Often times, one does not think much about the amount of money they are spending on an item when a credit card is used to make the purchase. Studies have proven that you think more about the cost of an item when paying by cash or debit card as the result is felt immediately with less money in your wallet and/or bank account. Many times you can use your debit card instead of your credit card whether purchasing an airline ticket or booking a hotel room. Begin by not using the credit card. If this is impossible for you, cut the card up so you won't have the opportunity to use it any longer. I am not going to tell you to pay off the credit card with the highest interest rate first or pay off the credit card with the smallest balance first as you need to make this decision. You know what will work best for you. Make certain that you are at least paying the minimum payment every month and the payment is made on time. You do not want to incur large late fees and the possibility that the finance charge rate will be increased due to a late payment. You may want to call the bank where you have your credit card and ask if you could have a lower finance rate as you are working to pay off the balance as soon as possible and if you have late payments on your account, a lower finance rate will not happen only a higher finance rate.

I would like to give you some examples of payments being made on your credit card and how the amount of money you pay each month does make a significant difference on the amount of time it takes you to pay off the credit card:

Example 1: Credit Card Balance of $7,103.14 with an Annual Percentage Rate of 8.24%. The Minimum Payment Due is $120.00 at this outstanding balance amount.

If you pay only the minimum payment each month, it will take you 24 years to pay off the balance in full and you will have paid approximately $11,718.09. Please keep in mind that this is without making any additional charges on the card.

If you are able to make a payment of $223.46 each month, it will take you 36 months to pay off the balance in full and you will have paid approximately $8,044.56. **(Savings = $3,673.53).**

This is a substantial savings just by paying more than the minimum each month. It may be difficult at the beginning to pay almost double the minimum payment but if you can do it, it is certainly worth it as you can see.

Example 2: Credit Card Balance of $19,989.50 with an Annual Percentage Rate of 14.98%. The Minimum Payment Due is $558.00 at this outstanding balance amount.

If you pay only the minimum payment each month, it will take you 4 years to pay off the balance in full and you will have paid approximately $26,650.73. Please keep in mind that this is without making any additional charges on the card.

If you are able to make a payment of $693.64 each month, it will take you 36 months to pay off the balance in full and you will have paid approximately $24,971.04. **(Savings = $1,679.69).**

Again, in this example we can see that a substantial savings is realized just by paying more than the minimum each month.

The most important thing in paying off credit card debt is to make the minimum payment and make certain that the payment is made on time. If you arc unable to pay more than the minimum at the beginning, do not be concerned about it but make it a goal to pay more than the minimum payment amount each month when you are able to do so.

Per the Good Morning America show on June 30, 2009, it is interesting to note that banks in general increased their overdraft fees, late fees on credit card payments and ATM fees for 2009. Banks overdraft fees were $25.00 in 2008 and were increased to $27.50 in 2009. In 2009, banks made **$39 Billion** in overdraft fees alone! Many of these overdraft fees were incurred when people forgot to record their debit card purchases in their check registers and the balance shown in their checkbook was higher then it actually was. It is important to remember to record your debit card purchases in your check register so not to be charged overdraft fees. I find it helpful to place the purchase receipt in my checkbook as a reminder to deduct it from my checkbook balance later that day. Fortunately, I have never failed to record the purchase and subtract the amount from my checkbook balance to date!!

As per the Bible, we read in Proverbs 22:7, "The rich ruleth over the poor, and the borrower is servant to the lender." Always remember that it is much easier to get into debt than it is to get out. It is important to keep in mind that we live in uncertain economic times. If you or your spouse lose your job, you still need to meet your financial obligations. If you have outstanding credit card debt, make it a priority to pay it off as soon as possible. I am sure you will sleep much better at night knowing that you have no credit card debt. We live in a very stressful world today and anxiety is common place; we do not need the added concern of how to pay our credit card debt when the household income is reduced due to the layoff of a job or perhaps someone in your household not being able to work for weeks or months due to an unexpected medical condition.

To conclude this chapter, keep in mind that **Cash is King**. It is best to save your money and purchase the item when you have the money to pay for it in cash or by the use of your debit card. This is what people did years ago. They saved their money and bought the item only when they could afford it. We need to get back to the good practice of paying for things with cash, the debit card or even by a credit card but only when the balances on a credit card can be paid in full every month. Americans need to stop living beyond their means by the use of the credit card. Layaway Plans are making a huge comeback with several retailers and layaway plans allow you to have more control of your money. You can pay for an item over time as the expense is allocated in your budget and when you take the item home, you own it. There are several stores that offer the layaway plan today such as Best Buy, Big Lots, Burlington Coat Factory, Kmart, Meijer, TJ Maxx and Toys R Us to name just a few; so, you may want to take advantage of this service as many people did years ago. We need to save more and spend less. Per the ABC Evening News on November 15, 2010, Diane Sawyer stated that Americans save a little over 5% of their incomes while the Chinese save 20% of their incomes. Many of us today are finding that we can live within our means and we are actually happier for doing so. The people who have been in credit card debt and worked hard to get out of it, do not want to go down that road again.

Chapter 3
Rich versus Poor

We are hearing much talk these days about how the middle class is shrinking and in the future there will only be two classes of people. You will either be rich or you will be poor. It is not possible for everyone to be in the rich category, but doesn't just knowing that if you are now middle class, you will either fall into the rich or poor class in the future motivate you enough to do something about it? One must take control of those things in life that we can and we must do it today. **There is no time to waste!** Below are the differences in the saving and spending habits of the rich versus the poor.

The Saving Habits of the Rich:

1. The rich delay gratification. They do not make major purchases until they have saved the money for them.

2. The rich invest their money in Stocks and Bonds, 401K Plans and Annuities, CDs at the Bank, and Savings Accounts, as well as Real Estate. Many people have

obtained their wealth by paying themselves first and they do this by having a certain percentage of their paycheck going directly into a Savings Account. Obviously, these people work off of a budget.

The Spending Habits of the Rich:

1. The rich pay their credit card balances off in full each month. They know they will have the money to pay for their purchases in 30 days and they use their credit card(s) wisely. The rich view the credit card as a great leverage tool. The rich do not pay high interest on credit cards.

2. The rich often buy expensive cars but the purchase price of the car is only a small percentage of their net worth. Many rich people see the car as a means of transportation only and drive only a modestly priced car. They feel they do not have to impress anyone and choose to drive whatever vehicle they want to.

3. Many times the rich do not pay a penny more for something then they have to; they love a bargain! The rich try to buy only when the item is on sale and they check the weekly supermarket flyers for the best prices on food items for the week.

Keep in mind that money gives you freedom and it gives you power. Many times the rich can use this power to command a good deal in the transaction.

4. The rich live below their means. They spend less than they earn.

The Saving Habits of the Poor:

1. The poor in general do not save much money and are convinced that they do not earn enough money to save on a regular basis. However, if the poor could lower their debt especially if they are paying high interest on credit card debt, I am sure they could find room in their budget to save even a small amount at the beginning. You just need to start and start today! Sit down and prepare a budget for yourself to assist you in attaining the saving goal you want to reach. If you cannot afford that new flat screen TV, do not put it on a credit card and pay high interest but rather save for it and purchase it with cash.

2. The poor invest in Savings Accounts, CDs at the Bank and a 401K Plan if they are fortunate enough to work for an employer who offers this but cannot always invest enough in the 401K Plan to receive the full match from the employer or even worse, cannot afford to contribute to the 401K Plan at all.

The Spending Habits of the Poor:

1. Unfortunately, the poor spend their money on the lotteries and have a tendency to gamble thinking they

will strike it rich. They need to keep in mind that very few people actually strike it rich playing the lotteries. They should take the money they spend on lottery tickets and put it in a Savings Account so that they will have their money working for them by earning interest on the money they would have most likely lost playing the lottery. Lotteries build false hope and people tend to put all of their hope and energy into winning the lottery and are disappointed most of the time. Also, this false hope prevents them from being motivated to earn the money that they need to live the lifestyle they want.

2. The poor live above their means. They spend more than they earn.

3. The poor use credit cards to purchase the items they want and do not pay off the balances each month. They do not want to save for the item and pay for it with cash. It is all about instant gratification!

4. The poor don't really pay close attention to how much they pay for an item; looking for the best price on an item is not something they find of interest. The poor have the tendency of buying a loaf of bread at the convenience store close by their home as opposed to buying it at a store at a much lower price.

To conclude this chapter, what category are you in at the present time and what category do you want to be in in the future? Taking control of your money matters will put you in more control of your life overall. Start working on a budget today! Get yourself motivated to being in control of the money matters in your household.

SEGMENT II

HEALTH MATTERS

Chapter 4
Cigarette Smoking

As I mentioned in Chapter 1, if you smoke, you need to quit **now**! The most important reason for quitting is not the expense of it but rather how bad cigarette smoking is for your health. There is absolutely nothing good about smoking. The United States Congress adopted the Federal Cigarette Labeling and Advertising Act of 1965 and the Public Health Cigarette Smoking Act of 1969. These two laws required a health warning on cigarette packages, banned cigarette advertising in the broadcasting media and called for an annual report on the health consequences of smoking. The health warning alone on packages should be enough to make people quit smoking. Unfortunately, people still smoke. I know you have heard that smoking is very bad for your health but this alone is not enough of a deterrent for people to quit or even for people never to begin smoking in the first place. I hope that by reading this chapter and the in-depth details about what smoking does to your body, you will be motivated enough to quit . Cigarette smoking is not only bad for the smoker's health but the health of those who breathe in the second-hand smoke as well. Thus, the reason that so many non-smokers complained about smoking being allowed in public places. Years ago, people did not give much thought to the negative implications of smoking and actors and actresses smoking in the movies even made it look glamorous. Take particular notice the next time you are watching an old movie and you will understand what I mean. However, smoking is not glamorous and it has many ill effects on the body which include Lung Cancer, Heart Disease, Throat Cancer and Emphysema.

Per the Centers for Disease Control website: http://www.cdc.gov/tobacco/data_statistics/fact-sheet:

Smoking causes death:

1. The adverse health effects from cigarette smoking account for an estimated 443,000 deaths, or nearly one of every five deaths each year in the United States. This equates to more than 1,200 people dying every day in the United States from smoking cigarettes.

2. More deaths are caused each year by tobacco use than by all deaths from human immunodeficiency virus (HIV), illegal drug use, alcohol use, motor vehicle injuries, suicides and murders combined.

3. Smoking causes 90% of all lung cancer deaths in men and 80% of all lung cancer deaths in women.

4. An estimated 90% of all deaths from chronic obstructive lung disease are caused by smoking.

The following information was found on the Centers for Disease Control (CDC) Website. http://www.cdc.gov/tobacco/data_statistics/sgr/2010

If you quit smoking, you will:

1. Prolong your life.

2. Reduce the risk of:
    a. Heart Disease
    b. High Blood Pressure
    c. Heart Attack
    d. Lung Cancer
    e. Throat Cancer
    f. Gum Disease
    g. Emphysema
    h. Ulcers

3. Feel Healthier. After quitting smoking, you won't cough as much, you will have fewer sore throats and you will have a higher energy level.

4. Look Better. Quitting can help you prevent face wrinkles, get rid of stained teeth and improve the look of your skin overall.

5. Improve your sense of taste and smell.

6. Save Money.

What is in Tobacco Smoke?

Cigarettes, Cigars and Pipe Tobacco are made from dried tobacco leaves, as well as ingredients added for flavor and other reasons. Tobacco smoke contains a deadly mix of more than 7,000 chemicals. Hundreds are toxic. About 70 can cause cancer.

A. Cancer-Causing Chemicals:

1. Formaldehyde - Used to embalm dead bodies.

2. Benzene - Found in Gasoline.

3. Polonium 210 - Radioactive and very toxic.

4. Vinyl Chloride - Used to make pipes.

B. Toxic Metals:

1. Chromium - Used to make steel.

2. Arsenic - Used in pesticides.

3. Lead - Once used in paint.

4. Cadmium - Used in making batteries.

C. Poison Gases:

1. Carbon Monoxide - Found in car exhaust.

2. Hydrogen Cyanide - Used in chemical weapons.

3. Ammonia - Used in household cleaners.

4. Butane - Used in lighter fluid.

5. Toluene - Found in paint thinners.

Per the U.S. Department of Health and Human Services - Office of the Surgeon General on 12.08.10:
http://www.surgeongeneral.gov/library/tobacco

A. There is no safe level of exposure to tobacco smoke. Any exposure to tobacco smoke even an occasional cigarette or exposure to secondhand smoke is harmful.

1. You don't have to be a heavy smoker or a long-time smoker to get a smoking-related disease or have a heart attack or asthma attack that is triggered by tobacco smoke.

2. Low levels of smoke exposure, including exposures to secondhand tobacco smoke lead to a rapid and sharp

increase in dysfunction and inflammation of the lining of the blood vessels which are implicated in heart attacks and stroke.

3. Tobacco smoke itself is a known human carcinogen.

4. Chemicals in tobacco smoke interfere with the functioning of fallopian tubes, increasing risk for adverse pregnancy outcomes such as ectopic pregnancy, miscarriage, and low birth weight. They also damage the DNA in sperm which might reduce fertility and harm fetal development.

B. Damage from tobacco smoke is immediate.

1. The chemicals in tobacco smoke reach your lungs quickly every time you inhale. Your blood then carries the toxicants to every organ in your body.

2. The chemicals and toxicants in tobacco smoke damage DNA, which can lead to cancer. Smoking causes about 85% of lung cancers in the United States.

3. Exposure to tobacco smoke quickly damages blood vessels throughout the body and makes blood more likely to clot. This damage can cause heart attacks, strokes, and even sudden death.

4. The chemicals in tobacco smoke inflame the delicate lining of the lungs and can cause permanent damage

that reduces the ability of the lungs to exchange air efficiently and leads to chronic obstructive pulmonary disease (COPD), which includes emphysema and chronic bronchitis.

C. Smoking longer means more damage.

1. Both the risk and the severity of many diseases caused by smoking are directly related to how long the smoker has smoked and the number of cigarettes smoked per day.

2. Chemicals in tobacco smoke cause inflammation and cell damage and can weaken the immune system. The body makes white blood cells to respond to injuries, infections and cancers. White blood cell counts stay high while smoking continues, meaning the body is constantly fighting against the damage caused by smoking which can lead to disease in almost any part of the body.

3. Smoking can cause cancer and weaken your body's ability to fight cancer. With any cancer, even those not related to tobacco use, smoking can decrease the benefits of chemotherapy and other cancer treatments. Exposure to tobacco smoke can help tumors grow.

4. The chemicals in tobacco smoke complicate the regulation of blood sugar levels, exacerbating the health issues resulting from diabetes. Smokers with diabetes have a higher risk of heart and kidney disease, amputation,

eye disease causing blindness, nerve damage and poor circulation.

D. Cigarettes are designed for addiction:

1. The design and contents of tobacco products make them more attractive and addictive than ever before. Cigarettes today deliver nicotine more quickly from the lungs to the heart and brain.

2. While nicotine is the key chemical compound that causes and sustains the powerful addicting effects of cigarettes, other ingredients and design features make them even more attractive and more addictive.

3. The powerful addicting elements of tobacco products affect multiple types of nicotine receptors in the brain.

4. Evidence suggests that psychosocial, biologic and genetic factors may also play a role in nicotine addiction.

5. Adolescents' bodies are more sensitive to nicotine, and adolescents are more easily addicted than adults. This helps explain why about 1,000 teenagers become daily smokers every day in the United States. Also, it is important to note that most current smokers became addicted as teenagers.

E. The only proven strategy for reducing the risk of tobacco-related disease and death is to never smoke, and if you do smoke to quit.

1. Quitting at any age and at any time is beneficial. It is never too late to quit, but the sooner the better.

2. Quitting gives your body a chance to heal the damage caused by smoking.

3. When smokers quit, the risk for a heart attack drops sharply after just 1 year; stroke risk can fall to about the same as a nonsmoker's after 2-5 years; risks for cancer of the mouth, throat, esophagus and bladder are cut in half after 5 years, and the risk of dying of lung cancer drops by half after 10 years.

4. Smokers often make several attempts before they are able to quit.

Why Quit Smoking?

1. Quitting smoking has major health benefits that start as soon as you quit.

2. Former smokers live longer than people who keep smoking.

3. Quitting smoking lowers the risk of lung cancer, other

cancers, heart attack, stroke and chronic diseases such as emphysema and chronic bronchitis.

4. Women who stop smoking before they get pregnant, or even during the first 3-4 months of pregnancy, reduce their risk of having a baby with low birth-weight to that of women who have never smoked.

A study done in 2008 in the United States gives a break-out of smokers by race as follows:

Whites 22.0%
African Americans 21.3%
Hispanics 15.8%
American Indians/Alaska Natives 32.4%
Asian Americans 9.9%

Also in 2008, the CDC reported almost 23.7% of those 25 to 44 years old were current smokers, compared with 9.3% of those aged 65 or older. As recently as 2007, nationwide, 20% of high school students smoked and 6% of middle school students smoked. In both high school and middle school, white and Hispanic students were more likely to smoke cigarettes than other races.

The next time you are tempted to light up a cigarette, remember that every cigarette you smoke, reduces your expected lifespan by 11 minutes. That means that 10 cigarettes a day for 10 years takes more than nine months off of your life.

Per the U.S. Department of Health and Human Services on November 10, 2010, in the United States: http://www.hhs.gov/secretary/aboutspeeches/sp201011

1. Every day nearly 4,000 kids under the age of 18 try their first cigarette.

2. Every day some 1,000 kids under the age of 18 become daily smokers.

3. Every day about 1,800 adults 18 and older become daily smokers.

4. There are 443,000 premature deaths annually in the United States due to smoking and second-hand smoke exposure. This is the leading preventable cause of death in America.

5. Smoking costs our health care system almost $100 billion per year.

6. Smoking costs almost another $100 billion per year in lost productivity.

7. Second-hand smoke in the United States costs more than $10 billion annually in health care expenditures.

Per the website http://www.cdc.gov/tobacco/ data statistics/fact sheet, secondhand smoke causes immediate harm to nonsmokers. If you are a nonsmoker, you should:

1. Not allow anyone to smoke in your home or near it.

2. Not allow anyone to smoke in your car even with the window down.

3. Make certain your children's day care centers and schools are tobacco free.

4. If your state allows smoking in public areas, look for restaurants and other places that do not allow smoking. "No-smoking sections" do not protect you and your family from secondhand smoke.

5. Teach your children to stay away from secondhand smoke. Be a good model by not smoking.

Is it any wonder that non-smokers do not want to be around smokers and pushed for mandatory smoking areas for smokers to smoke in. As of July 2010, 26 states have enacted statewide bans on smoking in all enclosed public places including bars and restaurants. However, there are 11 states with no statewide smoking ban. These states are:

Alabama
Alaska
Indiana
Kentucky
Mississippi
Missouri
Oklahoma
South Carolina
Texas
West Virginia
Wyoming

Highest Smoking Rate and the most Smoking Related Deaths in the U.S. are in the following states:

Kentucky
West Virginia
Nevada
Mississippi
Oklahoma
Tennessee
Arkansas
Alabama
Indiana
Missouri

Lowest Smoking Rate and the least Smoking Related Deaths in the U. S. are in the following states:

Utah
Hawaii

Smoking causes Lung Cancer. Smoking also causes the following lung diseases by damaging the airways and alveoli (small air sacs) of the lungs:

Emphysema
Bronchitis
Chronic Airway Obstruction (COPD)

Smoking causes the following cancers:

Acute Myeloid Leukemia
Bladder Cancer
Cancer of the Cervix
Cancer of the Esophagus
Kidney Cancer
Cancer of the Larynx (Voice Box)
Lung Cancer
Cancer of the Oral Cavity (Mouth)
Cancer of the Pancreas
Cancer of the Pharynx (Throat)
Stomach Cancer
Cancer of the Uterus

Women and Tobacco:

1. Cigarette smoking kills an estimated 178,000 women in the United States annually. The three leading smoking-related causes of death in women are:

Lung Cancer - 45,000
Heart Disease - 40,000
Chronic Lung Disease - 42,000

2. Smoking causes 90% of all lung cancer deaths in women. Since 1950, lung cancer deaths among women have increased by more than 600%. By 1987, lung cancer had surpassed breast cancer as the leading cause of cancer-related deaths in women.

3. Women who smoke have an increased risk for other cancers, including cancers of the oral cavity, pharynx, larynx, esophagus, pancreas, kidney, bladder and uterine cervix. Women who smoke double their risk for developing coronary heart disease and increase by more than tenfold their likelihood of dying from chronic obstructive pulmonary disease (COPD).

4. Cigarette smoking increases the risk for infertility, preterm delivery, stillbirth, low birth weight and sudden infant death syndrome (SIDS).

5. Postmenopausal women who smoke have lower bone density than women who have never smoked.

6. Women who smoke have an increased risk for hip fracture than women who have never smoked.

Per the Centers for Disease Control website, http://cdc. gov/tobacco/data_statistics/fact-sheet:

Men and Tobacco:

1. Men who smoke increase the risk of developing lung cancer by 23 times.

2. Smoking causes 90% of all lung cancer deaths in men.

3. Researchers have found that smoking might damage the DNA in men's sperm. This DNA damage might decrease fertility, cause birth defects, or lead to miscarriage.

Deaths Worldwide each Year due to Second-Hand Smoke:

Second-hand smoke kills more that 600,000 people worldwide every year per a new study by the World Health Organization's Tobacco-Free Initiative. This study was paid for by the Swedish National Board of Health and Welfare and Bloomberg Philanthropies. The results of this study were published in the British Medical Journal, Lancet on November 26, 2010. The researchers in this study analyzed data from the year

2004 for 192 countries. These are the findings of the study:

1. 40% of children regularly breathe in second-hand smoke.

2. 30% of non-smoking men and women regularly breathe in second-hand smoke.

3. Children whose parents smoke have a higher risk of Sudden Infant Death Syndrome, Ear Infections, Pneumonia, Bronchitis and Asthma. Also, their lungs may grow more slowly than kids whose parents don't smoke.

4. People living in Europe and Asia are exposed the most to second-hand smoke.

5. People living in the Americas, the Eastern Mediterranean and Africa are exposed the least to second-hand smoke.

Worldwide each Year, it is Estimated that Second-Hand Smoke Causes:

1. 379,000 deaths from heart disease.

2. 165,000 deaths from lower respiratory disease.

3. 36,900 deaths from asthma.

4. 21,400 deaths from lung cancer.

<u>Ways to Quit Smoking:</u>

1. Cold Turkey. This is quitting without any outside help. Only 10% of the people who try to quit this way, succeed on the first attempt.

2. Behavioral Therapy. This method involves meeting with a Therapist who will help you find the most effective way to quit.

3. Nicotine Replacement Therapy. This includes:
Nicotine Gum
Patches
Inhalers
Lozenges

If you are under the age of 18, you need your Doctor's permission to use nicotine replacement therapy.

4. Medicine. There are drugs such as Zyban and Chantix which are formulated to help people quit smoking. Your Doctor must prescribe these medications.

5. Combination Treatments.

Needless to say, quitting smoking is one of the hardest things to do yet one of the best things you can do for both your short-term and long-term health. Within hours of not smoking, your body begins to recover from the effects of nicotine and additives in cigarettes. Your blood pressure, heart rate, and body temperature, all of which are elevated due to the nicotine in cigarettes, return to healthier levels. Your lung capacity increases and the bronchial tubes relax making breathing much easier. Poisonous carbon monoxide in your blood decreases allowing the blood to carry more oxygen.

As I conclude this chapter, I sincerely hope that if you smoke, you will now have the motivation to quit based on the facts presented of what smoking does to your health. If one is fortunate enough to have good health, shouldn't we do everything in our power to retain that good health. And, if you are thinking about starting to smoke, I hope that after reading this chapter, you will no longer desire to begin the smoking habit at all. Perhaps you have loved ones who smoke. Consider giving them a copy of this book; it could prolong their life and wouldn't this be one of the greatest gifts you could give them.

Chapter 5
Drinking Alcohol

Alcohol is created when grains, fruits, or vegetables are fermented, a process that uses yeast or bacteria to change the sugars in the food into alcohol. The kind of alcohol that people drink is ethanol, which is a sedative. When alcohol is consumed, it's absorbed into a person's bloodstream. Alcohol then affects the central nervous system which controls all body functions. Alcohol actually blocks some of the messages trying to get to the brain. This alters a person's perceptions, emotions, movement, vision and hearing. Beer, wine and hard liquor contain different amounts of alcohol. Proof refers to the amount of alcohol in the liquor. For example, 40 proof liquor contains 20% alcohol. Traditional wine has approximately 8-14% alcohol and regular beer has 4-6% alcohol. The amount of alcohol that a person can drink safely is highly individual, depending on genetics, age, sex and family history.

Per the Centers for Disease Control website, http://www.cdc.gov/alcohol/fact-sheets/alcohol-US:

There are approximately 79,000 deaths attributable to excessive alcohol use each year in the United States. This makes excessive alcohol use the third leading lifestyle-related cause of death for the nation.

The Standard Measure of Alcohol.

In the United States, a standard drink is any drink that contains 0.6 ounces (13.7 grams or 1.2 tablespoons) of pure alcohol. Generally, this amount of pure alcohol is found in:

1. 12-ounces of regular beer or wine cooler.
2. 8-ounces of malt liquor.
3. 5-ounces of wine.
4. 1.5-ounces of 80 proof distilled spirits or liquor (e.g., gin, rum, vodka, whiskey).

Moderate Drinking

If you drink alcohol, do so in moderation.

For women, 1 drink per day.
For men, 2 drinks per day.

Heavy Drinking

For women, more than 1 drink per day on average.
For men, more than 2 drinks per day on average.

Binge Drinking

For women, 4 or more drinks during a single occasion.
For men, 5 or more drinks during a single occasion.

Most people who binge drink are not alcoholics or alcohol dependent.

Excessive Drinking

This includes heavy drinking, binge drinking or both.

People who should not drink alcohol at all:

1. Pregnant women or women trying to become pregnant.
2. People taking prescriptions or over-the-counter drugs that may cause harm if mixed with alcohol.
3. People younger than 21 years old.
4. People recovering from alcoholism.
5. People suffering from a medical condition that may worsen by drinking alcohol.
6. People driving or planning to drive.

Immediate Health Risks of Excessive Alcohol Use include:

1. Unintentional injuries including:
    a. Traffic injuries
    b. Falls
    c. Drowning
    d. Burns

e. Firearm injuries

2. Violence, including intimate partner violence and child maltreatment:
> a. About 35% of victims report that offenders are under the influence of alcohol.
> b. Alcohol use is also associated with 2 out of 3 incidents of intimate partner violence.
> c. Studies have also shown that alcohol is a leading factor in child maltreatment and neglect cases and is the most frequent substance abused among these parents.

3. Risky Sexual Behavior including:
> a. Unprotected sex
> b. Sex with multiple partners
> c. Increased risk of sexual assault

These behaviors can result in unintended pregnancy or sexually transmitted diseases.

4. Miscarriage and stillbirth among pregnant women and a combination of physical and mental birth defects among children that last throughout life.

5. Alcohol poisoning, a medical emergency that results from high blood alcohol levels that suppress the central nervous system and can cause loss of consciousness, low blood pressure and body temperature, coma, respiratory depression, or death.

Long-Term Health Risks

Over time, excessive alcohol use can lead to the development of chronic diseases, neurological impairments and social problems including but not limited to:

1. Neurological problems, including dementia, stroke and neuropathy.
2. Cardiovascular problems, including myocardial infarction, cardiomyopathy, atrial fibrillation and hypertension.
3. Psychiatric problems, including depression, anxiety and suicide.
4. Social problems, including unemployment, lost productivity, and family problems.
5. Cancer of the mouth, throat, esophagus, liver, colon and breast. In general, the risk of cancer increases with increasing amounts of alcohol.
6. Liver diseases including-
    a. Alcoholic hepatitis
    b. Cirrhosis which is among the 15 leading causes of all deaths in the United States.
7. Among persons with Hepatitis C virus, worsening of liver function and interference with medications used to treat this condition.
8. Other gastrointestinal problems, including pancreatitis and gastritis.

Per the Centers for Disease Control website, http://www.cdc.gov/alcohol/fact-sheets/binge-drinking:

Binge drinking is a common pattern of excessive alcohol

use in the United States. The National Institute on Alcohol Abuse and Alcoholism defines binge drinking as a pattern of drinking that brings a person's blood alcohol concentration (BAC) to 0.08 grams percent or above. For men, this is 5 drinks or more in about 2 hours. For women, this is 4 drinks or more in about 2 hours. Most people who binge drink are not alcohol dependent.

Binge drinking is associated with many health problems, including-

1. Unintentional injuries (e.g., car crashes, falls, burns, drowning).
2. Intentional injuries (e.g., firearm injuries, sexual assault, domestic violence).
3. Alcohol poisoning.
4. Sexually transmitted diseases.
5. Unintended pregnancy.
6. Children born with Fetal Alcohol Spectrum Disorders.
7. High blood pressure, stroke and other cardiovascular diseases.
8. Liver disease.
9. Neurological damage.
10. Sexual dysfunction.
11. Poor control of diabetes.

Per the Centers for Disease Control website, http:// www.cdc.gov/alcohol/fact-sheets/men's health:

1. Men are more likely than women to drink excessively.

2. Men are more likely than women to take other risks (e.g., drive fast or without safety belts) when combined with excessive drinking, further increasing their risk of injury or death.
3. Excessive alcohol use can interfere with testicular function and male hormone production resulting in impotence, infertility, and reduction of male secondary sex characteristics such as facial hair and chest hair.
4. Alcohol consumption increases the risk of cancer of the mouth, throat, esophagus, liver and colon in men.

Per the Centers for Disease Control website, http://www.cdc.gov/alcohol/fact-sheets/women's health:

Although men are more likely to drink alcohol and drink in larger amounts, gender differences in body structure and chemistry cause women to absorb more alcohol and take longer to break it down and remove it from their bodies (i.e., to metabolize it). In other words, upon drinking equal amounts, women have higher alcohol levels in their blood than men, and the immediate effects occur more quickly and last longer.

National surveys show that about 6 out of every 10 women of child-bearing age (i.e., aged 18-44 years) use alcohol and slightly less than one third of women who drink alcohol in this age group binge drink.

In 2008, about 7.2% of pregnant women used alcohol.

Excessive drinking may disrupt menstrual cycling and

increase the risk of infertility, miscarriage, stillbirth and premature delivery.

Women who binge drink are more likely to have unprotected sex and multiple partners. These activities increase the risks of unintended pregnancy and sexually transmitted diseases.

Alcohol and Pregnancy:

1. Women who drink alcohol while pregnant increase their risk of having a baby with Fetal Alcohol Spectrum Disorders (FASD). The most severe form is Fetal Alcohol Syndrome (FAS), which causes mental retardation and birth defects.

2. FASD are completely preventable if a woman does not drink while pregnant or while she may become pregnant.

3. Studies have shown that about 1 of 20 pregnant women drank excessively before finding out they were pregnant. No amount of alcohol is safe to drink during pregnancy.

4. Research suggests that women who drink alcohol while pregnant are more likely to have a baby die from Sudden Infant Death Syndrome (SIDS). This risk substantially increases if a woman binge drinks during her first trimester of pregnancy.

5. The risk of miscarriage is also increased if a woman drinks excessively during her first trimester of pregnancy.

Other Health Concerns:

1. Liver Disease. The risk of cirrhosis and other alcohol-related liver diseases is higher for women than for men.

2. Impact on the Brain. Excessive drinking may result in memory loss and shrinkage of the brain. Research suggests that women are more vulnerable than men to the brain damaging effects of excessive alcohol use and the damage tends to appear with shorter periods of excessive drinking for women than for men.

3. Impact on the Heart. Studies have shown that women who drink excessively are at increased risk for damage to the heart muscle than men even for women drinking at lower levels.

4. Cancer. Alcohol consumption increases the risk of cancer of the mouth, throat, esophagus, liver, colon and breast among women. The risk of breast cancer increases as alcohol use increases.

5. Sexual Assault. Binge drinking is a risk factor for sexual assault, especially among young women in college settings. Each year, about 1 in 20 college women are sexually assaulted.

Per the Centers for Disease Control website, http://www.cdc.gov/alcohol/fact-sheets/underage

Underage Drinking

Alcohol use by persons under the age of 21 years is a major public health problem. Alcohol is the most commonly used and abused drug among youth in the United States, more than tobacco and illicit drugs. **Although drinking by persons under the age of 21 is illegal, people aged 12 to 20 years drink 11% of all alcohol consumed in the United States.** More than 90% of this alcohol is consumed in the form of binge drinks. In 2008, there were approximately 190,000 emergency room visits by persons under age 21 for injuries and other conditions linked to alcohol.

Drinking Levels among Youth

The 2009 Youth Risk Behavior Survey found that among high school students, during the past 30 days:

1. 42% drank some amount of alcohol.
2. 24% binge drank.
3. 10% drove after drinking alcohol.
4. 28% rode with a driver who had been drinking alcohol.

Consequences of Underage Drinking

Youth who drink alcohol are more likely to experience:

1. School problems, such as higher absence and poor or failing grades.

2.   Social problems, such as fighting and lack of participation in youth activities.
3. Legal problems, such as arrest for driving or physically hurting someone while drunk.
4. Physical problems, such as hangovers or illnesses.
5.   Unwanted, unplanned, and unprotected sexual activity.
6.   Disruption of normal growth and sexual development.
7. Physical and sexual assault.
8. Higher risk for suicide and homicide.
9. Alcohol-related car crashes and other unintentional injuries, such as burns, falls and drowning.
10. Memory problems.
11. Abuse of other drugs.
12. Changes in brain development that may have life-long effects.
13. Death from alcohol poisoning.

Youth who start drinking before age 15 years are five times more likely to develop alcohol dependence or abuse later in life than those who begin drinking at or after age 21 years.

To conclude this chapter, Alcoholism is a very serious matter. It not only can destroy the life of the alcoholic but the lives of their family members as well. Many times, the alcoholic puts all of their time, energy and money into their drinking addiction which in turn leaves their family with no money for food and other necessities in life. Many families are broken up due to the father or mother being an alcoholic. Often times, the alcoholic loses his job due

Pauline Parsons

to not showing up for work on time or not showing up for work at all. The thing to remember is that if you choose to drink, please drink in moderation. And most importantly, do not drink and drive!

Chapter 6
Obesity

The following information was obtained on the National Institutes of Health website: http://health.nih.gov/topics/obesity

Obesity is a term used to describe body weight that is much greater than what is considered healthy. If you are obese, you have a much higher amount of body fat than is healthy or desirable.

Adults with a body mass index (BMI) calculated as weight in kilograms divided by height in meters squared greater than 25 kg/m2 but less than 30kg/m2 are considered overweight.

Adults with a BMI greater than 30 kg/m2 are considered obese. Anyone who is more than 100 pounds overweight or who has a BMI greater than 40 kg/m2 is considered morbidly obese.

<u>Consuming more calories than you burn leads to being overweight and eventually obesity. The body stores unused calories as fat. Obesity can be the result of:</u>

1. Eating more food than your body can use.
2. Drinking too much alcohol.
3. Not getting enough exercise.
4. An underactive thyroid (hypothyroidism) may lead to weight gain, but usually only 5-10 pounds of weight.
5. Some antidepressants and antipsychotic medicines may also contribute to weight gain and obesity.
6. Sleep Deprivation. If you do not get enough sleep each night, you are increasing your risk of obesity.

<u>People who are at a higher risk for obesity:</u>

1. Lower income groups
2. Former smokers
3. People with chronic mental illness
4. People with disabilities
5. People with a sedentary lifestyle

Even modest weight loss can improve your health. A combination of dieting and exercise appears to work better than either one alone. When dieting, your main goal should be to learn new healthy ways of eating and make them a part of your everyday routine. Remember that if you drop pounds slowly and steadily, you are more likely to keep them off permanently.

<u>There are several behavioral changes that can have an impact on your weight loss success:</u>

1. Eat only at the table. No snacking in front of the TV.
2. Learn about appropriate portion sizes.
3. Choose low-calorie snacks such as raw vegetables over potato chips.
4. Consider learning meditation or yoga as a way of managing stress, rather than snacking.
5. Find ways to socialize and enjoy your family and friends that don't involve a meal or dessert.
6. Consider keeping a diet and exercise journal.
7. Join a support group.

Exercise is a major mood lifter, a great way to burn energy and a way to strengthen your bones. Exercise can also help you manage high blood pressure, heart disease or diabetes. Avoid a sedentary lifestyle by increasing your activity level in the following ways:

1. Perform aerobic exercise for at least 30 minutes a day, three times a week.
2. Increase your physical activity by walking rather than driving.
3. Take the stairs as opposed to using an elevator or an escalator.
4. Always talk to your health care provider before starting an exercise program.

Weight-loss surgery may be an option if you are very obese and have not been able to lose weight through diet and exercise. Be aware that these surgeries are not a "quick fix" for obesity. You must still be committed to diet and exercise after the surgery. The two most common weight-loss surgeries are:

1. Laparoscopic Gastic Banding. In this procedure, the surgeon places a band around the upper part of your stomach, creating a small pouch to hold food. The band limits the amount of food you can eat by making you feel full after eating small amounts of food.

2. Gastric Bypass Surgery. Helps you lose weight by changing how your stomach and small intestine handle the food you eat. After the surgery, you will not be able to eat as much as before, and your body will not absorb all the calories and other nutrients from the food you eat.

Per the Centers for Disease Control website, http://
www.cdc.gov/healthyweight:

When it comes to weight loss, there's no lack of fad
diets promising fast results. But such diets limit your
nutritional intake, can be unhealthy, and tend to fail in
the long run.

The key to achieving and maintaining a healthy weight
isn't about short-term dietary changes. It's about a lifestyle
that includes healthy eating, regular physical activity and
balancing the number of calories you consume with the
number of calories your body uses.

Staying in control of your weight contributes to good
health now and as you age.

Per the Centers for Disease Control website, http://
www.cdc.gov/vitalsigns/adultobesity/latest-findings:

1. Obesity means having excess body fat. Obesity is
   defined by body mass index or, BMI, which is
   calculated from your height and weight.
2. BMI greater than or equal to 30 means you are
   obese.
3. Non-Hispanic black women and Hispanics have the
   highest rates of obesity (41.9% and 30.7%).
4. Obesity is a contributing cause of many other health
   problems, including heart disease, stroke, diabetes
   and some types of cancer. Obesity can cause sleep
   apnea and breathing problems and make activity more
   difficult. Obesity can also cause problems during

pregnancy or make it more difficult for a woman to become pregnant.

5. Obese persons require more costly medical care. This places a huge financial burden on our medical care system.

Why is this epidemic happening?

1. Weight gain occurs when people eat too much food and get too little physical activity.
2. Societal and community changes have accompanied the rise in obesity.
3. People eat differently -
    a. Some Americans have less access to stores and markets that provide healthy, affordable food such as fruits and vegetables, especially in rural, minority and lower-income neighborhoods.
    b. There is too much sugar in our diet. Six out of ten adults drink at least 1 surgery drink per day.
    c. It is often easier and cheaper to get less healthy foods and beverages.
    d. Foods high in sugar, fat and salt are highly advertised and marketed.
4. Many communities are built in ways that make it difficult or unsafe to be physically active.
    a. Access to parks and recreation centers may be difficult or lacking and public transportation may
    not be available.
    b. Safe routes for walking or biking to school, work or play may not exist.

c. Too few students get quality, daily physical education in school.

Per the Centers for Disease Control website, http://www.cdc.gov/obesity/childhood/index:

Obesity is a serious health concern for children and adolescents. Results from the 2007-2008 National Health and Nutrition Examination Survey (NHANES), using measured heights and weights, indicate that an estimated 17% of children and adolescents ages 2-19 years are obese.

Among pre-school age children 2-5 years of age, obesity increased from 5 to 10.4% between 1976-1980 and 2007-2008 and from 6.5 to 19.6% among 6-11 year olds. Among adolescents aged 12-19, obesity increased from 5 to 18.1% during the same period.

Obese children and adolescents are at risk for health problems during their youth and as adults. Also, obese children and adolescents are more likely to become obese as adults.

Pauline Parsons

The following information was obtained on the website aarp.org: http://www.aarp.org/health

Obesity is a growing problem in the United States. Today, 72 million people are obese. Not only is obesity bad for your health but it is bad for your budget as well. On average, obese people spend $732 more per year on medical expenses than those with normal weight according to a 2009 study sponsored by the U.S. Agency for Healthcare Research and Quality. Also, obese workers are paid less than other workers.

Obesity cost as much as $147 billion each year in the United States according to the CDC. Per the CDC, in 2009, there were nine states within the U.S. where 1 in every 3 residents were obese. These states are Alabama, Arkansas, Kentucky, Louisiana, Mississippi, Missouri, Oklahoma, Tennessee and West Virginia. The states with the lowest obesity per resident were Colorado and Washington, D.C. with 1 in 5 residents classified as obese.

Per the cdc.gov website, Childhood obesity has more than tripled in the past 30 years. Childhood obesity is of major concern worldwide and First Lady Michelle Obama wants kids eating healthier and is raising awareness of childhood obesity through her campaign "Let's Move."

In conclusion, obesity is a serious health issue and should not be looked at simply as a cosmetic problem. If you are overweight or obese, I hope you will try diligently to eat healthier foods and exercise more. Best of luck with losing those extra pounds and being the healthier for it.

Chapter 7
Diabetes

Per the Centers for Disease Control website, http://www.cdc.gov/diabetes

The CDC projects that 1 in 3 people in America will have diabetes by the year 2050. Americans need to make immediate changes in their diet, physical activity, stress levels and amount of sleep they receive each night as all of these factors are known to decrease diabetes and obesity.

Diabetes remains the leading cause of new cases of blindness under the age of 75, as well as, kidney failure and preventable leg and foot amputation among adults in the United States.

People diagnosed with diabetes have medical costs that are more than twice that of people who do not have diabetes. The total cost of diabetes in the United States is estimated at $174 billion annually.

According to the International Diabetes Federation, there are about 285 million people worldwide that have diabetes in 2010 and 438 million people could have diabetes by 2030.

Today about 24 million Americans have diabetes and nearly 25% of them don't even know it.

<u>Contributing risk factors to developing Type 2 Diabetes are:</u>

1. Older Age

2. Obesity

3. Sedentary Lifestyle

4. Family History

5. Developing Diabetes while pregnant

6. Race/Ethnicity

<u>The Race/Ethnicity groups at increased risk are:</u>

1. African Americans
2. Hispanics/Latinos
3. American Indians/Alaska Natives
4. Some Asian-Americans and Pacific Islanders

This information was obtained from the National Diabetes Information Clearinghouse (NDIC) website: http://www.diabetes.niddk.nih.gov

First of all, what is Diabetes? Diabetes is a disorder of metabolism. Most of the food people eat is broken down into glucose, the form of sugar in the blood. Glucose is the main source of fuel for the body.

After digestion, glucose passes into the bloodstream where it is used by cells for growth and energy. There must be insulin present for the glucose to get into the cells. Insulin is a hormone produced by the pancreas, a large gland behind the stomach. When people eat, the pancreas automatically produces the right amount of insulin to move the glucose from the blood into the cells. With people who have diabetes, the pancreas either produces little or no insulin or the cells do not respond appropriately to the insulin that is produced. Glucose builds up in the blood, overflows into the urine and passes out of the body in the urine. As a result, the body loses its main source of fuel even though the blood contains large amounts of glucose.

There are 3 main types of diabetes:

1. Type 1 Diabetes

2. Type 2 Diabetes

3. Gestational Diabetes

Type 1 Diabetes. Type 1 Diabetes is an autoimmune disease. An autoimmune disease results when the body's system for fighting infection - the immune system - turns against a part of the body. In diabetes, the immune system attacks and destroys the insulin-producing beta cells in the pancreas. The pancreas then produces little or no insulin. A person who has Type 1 Diabetes must take insulin daily to live.

At the present time, scientists do not know exactly what causes the body's immune system to attack the beta cells. Type 1 Diabetes accounts for about 5-10% of diagnosed diabetes in the United States. Type 1 Diabetes develops most often in children and young adults but can appear at any age.

Symptoms of Type 1 Diabetes include increased thirst and urination, constant hunger, weight loss, blurred vision and extreme fatigue. If not diagnosed and treated with insulin, a person having Type 1 Diabetes can lapse into a life threatening diabetic coma.

Type 2 Diabetes. Type 2 Diabetes is the most common form of diabetes. About 90% to 95% of people who have diabetes have the Type 2. This form of diabetes is most often associated with older age, obesity, family history of diabetes, previous history of gestational diabetes and physical inactivity. About 80% of people with type 2 diabetes are overweight.

Type 2 Diabetes is increasingly being diagnosed in children and adolescents, especially among African-American, Mexican-American and Pacific Islander youth.

The symptoms of Type 2 Diabetes develop gradually. Their onset is not as sudden as in Type 1 Diabetes. Symptoms include fatigue, frequent urination, increased thirst and hunger, weight loss, blurred vision and slow healing of wounds or sores. Some people have no symptoms.

Gestational Diabetes. Some women develop gestational diabetes late in pregnancy. This form of diabetes usually disappears after the birth of the baby. Women who have had gestational diabetes run a 40 to 60 percent chance of developing type 2 diabetes within 5 to 10 years. About 3 to 8 percent of pregnant women in the United States develop gestational diabetes. Gestational diabetes is caused by the hormones of pregnancy or a shortage of insulin. Women with gestational diabetes may not experience any symptoms.

There are other types of diabetes but these three just mentioned are the most prevalent.

How is diabetes diagnosed? The fasting blood glucose test is the preferred test for diagnosing diabetes in children and non pregnant adults. The test is most reliable when done in the morning.

What is pre-diabetes? People with pre-diabetes have blood glucose levels that are higher than normal but not high enough for diagnosis of diabetes. This condition raises the risk of developing Type 2 Diabetes, Heart Disease and Stroke. Pre-diabetes is becoming more common in the United States. Those with pre-diabetes are likely to develop Type 2 Diabetes within 10 years unless they take steps to prevent or delay diabetes. People with pre-diabetes can do a lot to prevent or delay diabetes. One thing that people can do is lose 5 to 7 percent of their body weight through diet and physical activity. It isn't necessary to join a gym, one can simply walk for at least 30 minutes each day, 5 days a week.

Take Note: Impact of Diabetes on your Health:

Diabetes is associated with long-term complications that affect almost every part of the body. The disease often leads to blindness, heart and blood vessel disease, stroke, kidney failure, amputations and nerve damage.

<u>Take Note: Impact of Diabetes in the United States:</u>

1. It affects 23.6 million people in the U.S. which is 7.8% of the population.

2. It is a leading cause of death and disability.

3. It costs $174 billion per year.

If you experience any of the symptoms of Type 1 or Type 2 Diabetes, make an appointment with an Endocrinologist as soon as possible.

In conclusion of this chapter on Diabetes, you have just read of the many health issues related to diabetes. One must do everything they can to prevent having diabetes, especially if you come from a family history of diabetes. If you are overweight, you should plan to lose a few pounds right away and to exercise more. You need to make a healthier diet and regular exercise as part of your daily regimen. You do have control over whether or not you chose to have a healthier diet and exercise routine in your daily living. You must take control of this aspect of your life.

Chapter 8
Stroke

Per the cdc.gov website: http://www.cdc.gov/stroke

1. A stroke occurs when a clot blocks the blood supply to the brain or when a blood vessel in the brain bursts.

2. Stroke is the third leading cause of death in the United States. Around 137,000 people die in the US from strokes every year.

3. Someone in the United States has a stroke every 40 seconds. Every 3 to 4 minutes someone dies of a stroke.

4. Stroke is a leading cause of death for both men and women.

5. About 795,000 people in the United States have a stroke every year; about 610,000 of which are new strokes. About 185,000 people who survive a stroke will eventually have another one.

6. Stroke is an important cause of disability.

7. In 2010, stroke will cost the United States $73.7 billion. This total includes the cost of health care services, medications and lost productivity.

The Risk Factors for a Stroke:

1. High Blood Pressure (Hypertension)
2. High Cholesterol
3. Diabetes
4. Smoking
5. Increasing Age

Some common warning signs and symptoms of a stroke are:

1. Sudden numbness or weakness of the face, arm or leg, especially on one side of the body.

2. Sudden confusion, trouble speaking or understanding.

3. Sudden trouble seeing in one eye or both eyes.

4. Sudden trouble walking, dizziness, loss of balance or coordination.

5. Sudden severe headache with no known cause.

You are not able to control some of the risk factors for stroke such as heredity, age or gender, but keep in mind that there are some risk factors that you do have control of such as not smoking, not drinking excessively, and getting plenty of exercise.

How is a stroke diagnosed?

A stroke is a medical emergency. One should first call 911 and have an ambulance arrive as soon as possible. The affected person should lie flat to promote an optimal blood flow to the brain.

The Rehabilitation Process after having a stroke includes:

1. Speech Therapy to relearn talking and swallowing.

2. Occupational Therapy to regain dexterity in the arms and hands.

3. Physical Therapy to improve strength and walking.

4. Family education to orient the family in caring for their loved one at home and the challenges they will face.

In conclusion, stroke is a serious health condition in the United States and worldwide. The risk factors for having a stroke are noted above. Please take a second glance at the risk factors and if any of them apply to you, take immediate action on making changes so that you do everything in your power to prevent a stroke from happening to you.

Chapter 9
Heart Disease

Per the CDC website: http://www.cdc.gov/HeartDisease/ facts

1. Heart Disease is the leading cause of death for both men and women in the United States.

2. In 2006, 631,636 people died from heart disease. Heart disease caused 26% of deaths - more than 1 in every 4 people in the United States.

3. In 2006, the state with the highest deaths due to heart disease was Mississippi and the state with the lowest deaths was Minnesota.

4. Coronary Artery Disease is the most common form of heart disease. In 2005, 445,687 people died from coronary heart disease.

5. Every year, 785,000 Americans have their first heart attack. Another 470,000 Americans who have already had one or two heart attacks have another heart attack.

6. In 2010, heart disease will cost the United States $316.4 billion. This total includes the cost of health care services, medications and lost productivity.

7. Who is at the greatest risk for developing Heart Disease? The Risk Factor % for US adults during the year 2005-2006 were:

Inactivity	**39.5%**
Obesity	**33.9%**
High Blood Pressure	**30.5%**
Cigarette Smoking	**20.8%**
High Cholesterol	**15.6%**
Diabetes	**10.1%**

Per the website, cdc.gov, the five major Symptoms of a Heart Attack are:

1. Pain or discomfort in the jaw, neck or back.

2. Feeling weak, light-headed or faint.

3. Chest pain or discomfort.

4. Pain or discomfort in the arms or shoulder.

5. Shortness of breath.

If you think you or someone you know is having a heart attack, call 911 immediately. A person's chances of surviving a heart attack are greatly increased if emergency treatment is given to the victim as soon as possible.

Heart Disease in Men:

1. Heart Disease is the leading cause of death for men in the United States.

2. Heart Disease killed 26% of the men who died in 2006, more than 1 in every 4.

3. Half of the men who die suddenly of coronary heart disease have no previous symptoms.

4. Between 70% and 89% of sudden cardiac events occur in men.

Heart Disease in Women:

1. Heart Disease is the leading cause of death for women in the United States.

2. Heart Disease killed 26% of the women who died in 2006, more than 1 in every 4.

3. Heart Disease is often thought to be a "man's disease," yet about the same amount of men and women die each year from heart disease in the United States.

4. Almost 2/3 of all women who die suddenly from coronary heart disease have no previous symptoms.

In conclusion, Heart Disease is the leading cause of death in the United States for both men and women. Americans need to do whatever they can to reduce their risk of developing heart disease. If you have any of the risk factors listed above, you need to be proactive and get yourself in better health immediately. Your health is worth it! You do have control of what you eat and whether or not you exercise on a regular basis, as well as, choosing to smoke cigarettes.

Chapter 10
Best Foods For Your Heart

Per the Health Finder website, http://www.healthfinder. gov/prevention/viewtool:

Tips for a Healthy Heart:

1. Eat less saturated and trans fat. Stay away from fatty meats, fried foods, cakes and cookies.
2. Cut down on sodium (salt). Look for the low-sodium or "no salt added" brands of canned soups, vegetables, snack foods and lunch meats.
3. Get more fiber. Fiber is in vegetables, fruits and whole grains.

Fruits and Vegetables:

Choose fruits and vegetables in different colors. Buy them in season to save money.

1. Fresh fruits such as apples, oranges, bananas, pears and peaches.
2. Canned fruit in 100% juice, not syrup.
3. Dried fruit.

4. Frozen berries without added sugar.
5. Fresh vegetables such as tomatoes, cabbage, broccoli and spinach.
6. Leafy greens for salads.
7. Canned vegetables low in sodium (salt).
8. Frozen vegetables without added butter or sauces.

Milk and Milk Products:

1. Fat-free or low-fat (1%) milk.
2. Cheese (3 grams of fat or less per serving).
3. Fat-free or low-fat yogurt.

Bread, Cereals and Grains:

1. 100% whole wheat bread.
2. Whole-grain breakfast cereals (such as oatmeal).
3. Grains such as brown rice, barley and bulgur.
4. Whole wheat or whole-grain pasta.
5. Popcorn.

Meat, Beans, Eggs and Nuts:

1. Fish.
2. Chicken and turkey breast, without skin.
3. Beef: round, sirloin, tenderloin and extra lean ground beef.
4. Pork: leg, shoulder and tenderloin.
5. Beans, lentils, dried peas.
6. Eggs and egg substitutes.
7. Nuts and seeds.

Fats and Oils:

To cut back on fat, try cooking with a non-stick cooking spray.

1. Margarine and spreads with no trans fats (soft, tub or liquid).
2. Vegetable oil (canola, olive, peanut, sesame oil).
3. Light or fat-free salad dressing and mayonnaise.
4. Non-stick cooking spray.

Chapter 11
High Blood Pressure

Per the Centers for Disease Control website, http://www.cdc.gov/bloodpressure:

About 1 in 3 adults in the United States has high blood pressure, which increases the risk for heart disease and stroke, the first and third leading causes of death in the United States.

Blood pressure is the force of blood against your artery walls as it circulates through your body. Blood pressure normally rises and falls throughout the day, but it can cause health problems if it stays high for a long time.

Blood pressure is measured using two numbers. The first (systolic) number represents the pressure in your blood vessels when your heart beats. The second (diastolic) number represents the pressure in your vessels when your heart rests between beats. If the measurement reads 120 systolic and 80 diastolic, you would say "120 over 80".

Effects of High Blood Pressure:

High blood pressure can damage your health in many ways. It can harden the arteries, decreasing the flow of blood and oxygen to the heart. This reduced flow can cause -

1. Chest Pain also called angina.
2. Heart Failure, which occurs when the heart can't pump enough blood and oxygen to your other organs.
3. Heart Attack, which occurs when the blood supply to your heart is blocked and heart muscle cells die from a lack of oxygen. The longer the blood flow is blocked, the greater the damage to the heart.

High Blood Pressure can burst or block arteries that supply blood and oxygen to the brain, causing a stroke. People of all ages and backgrounds can develop high blood pressure and it's preventable.

America's High Blood Pressure Burden:

1. 31.3% of U.S. adults have high blood pressure.
2. High Blood Pressure is a major risk factor for heart disease, stroke, congestive heart failure and kidney disease.
3. High Blood Pressure was listed as a primary or contributing cause of death for 326,000 Americans in 2006.
4. In 2010, high blood pressure will cost the United States $76.6 Billion in health care services, medications, and missed days of work.

5. About 70% of those with high blood pressure and took medication had their high blood pressure controlled. The control rate was 46.6% among all hypertensive patients.
6. 25% of American adults have pre-hypertension-blood pressure numbers that are higher than normal, but not yet in the high blood pressure range.

Women are about as likely as men to develop high blood pressure during their lifetimes. However, for people under 45 years old, the condition affects more men than women. For people 65 years and older, it affects more women than men. African Americans develop high blood pressure more often, and at an earlier age than whites and Mexican Americans do. Among African Americans, more women than men have the condition. Blood pressure tends to rise as people get older; so, everyone's risk for high blood pressure increases with age. In addition, some medical conditions can also raise your risk of high blood pressure such as -

1. Pre-hypertension - blood pressure levels that are slightly higher than normal increases the risk that you will go on to develop chronic high blood pressure.
2. Diabetes - about 60% of people who have diabetes also have high blood pressure.

Lifestyle

1. Eat a healthy diet. Eating healthy can help keep your blood pressure down. Eat lots of fresh fruits and vegetables which provide nutrients such as potassium and fiber. Also, eat foods that are low in saturated fat and cholesterol. Avoid sodium by limiting the amount of salt you add to your food. Be aware that many processed foods and restaurant meals are high in sodium. Studies have shown that people who eat a healthy diet can lower their blood pressure.

2. Maintain a healthy weight. Being overweight can raise your blood pressure. Losing weight can help you lower your blood pressure.

3. Be physically active. Physical activity can help lower blood pressure. The Surgeon General recommends that adults should engage in moderate physical activities for at least 30 minutes on most days of the week.

4. Don't smoke. Smoking injures blood vessels and speeds up the hardening of the arteries. Further, smoking is a major risk for heart disease and stroke.

5. Limit Alcohol Use. Drinking too much alcohol is associated with high blood pressure. If you drink alcohol, you should do so in moderation-no more than one drink per day for women or two drinks per day for men.

Chapter 12
High Cholesterol

Per the Centers for Disease Control website, http://www.cdc.gov/cholesterol:

Having high blood cholesterol puts you at risk for heart disease, the leading cause of death in the United States. About 1 of every 6 adult Americans has high blood cholesterol.

Cholesterol is a waxy, fat-like substance that your body needs. But, when you have too much in your blood, it can build up on the walls of your arteries. This can lead to heart disease and stroke. There are no symptoms of high cholesterol. Many people have never had their cholesterol checked; so, they don't know they are at risk. A simple blood test can tell you your level. The good news is that there are steps you can take to prevent high cholesterol or to reduce your levels if they are high:

1. Diet. Certain foods raise your cholesterol levels. These foods tend to contain saturated fats, trans fatty acids (trans fats), dietary cholesterol, or triglycerides.

2. Weight. Being overweight can raise LDL, lower HDL and raise total cholesterol levels.

3. Physical Inactivity. Not getting enough exercise can make you gain weight which can lead to increased cholesterol levels.

Key Definitions:

Cholesterol is a fat-like substance in the body. High levels in the blood can lead to heart disease and stroke.

LDL ("bad") cholesterol makes up the majority of the cholesterol in the body. Too much LDL can lead to heart disease.

HDL ("good") cholesterol reduces the risk for heart disease. Scientists think that HDL mops up bad cholesterol and carries it to the liver which then flushes it from the body.

Saturated Fats come largely from animal fat in the diet, but also from some vegetable oils such as palm oil.

Trans Fats come from vegetable oil that has been hardened by a process called hydrogenation. Many snack foods, fast foods and baked goods contain trans fats.

Dietary Cholesterol occurs in foods that come from animal sources, including egg yolks, meat and dairy products.

Triglycerides are another type of fat in food. As with cholesterol, having high levels of triglycerides can raise a person's risk for heart disease.

Heredity. High Cholesterol can run in families.

High Cholesterol usually has no signs or symptoms. Only a doctor's check will reveal it. You doctor can do a simple blood test to check your cholesterol levels.

What You Can Do:

1. Eat a healthy diet.
2. Maintain a healthy weight.
3. Exercise regularly.
4. Don't smoke.
5. Treat high cholesterol.

Chapter 13
Effects of Sleep Deprivation on the Body

<u>**Per the Centers for Disease Control website,**</u> http://www.cdc.gov/sleep/about_sleep/chronic

Insufficient sleep has been linked to the development and management of a number of chronic diseases and conditions, including diabetes, cardiovascular disease, obesity and depression.

Diabetes. Research has found that insufficient sleep is linked to an increased risk for the development of Type 2 diabetes.

Cardiovascular Disease. Persons with sleep apnea have found to be at an increased risk for a number of cardiovascular diseases. Notably, hypertension, stroke, coronary heart disease and irregular heartbeats have been found to be more common among those with disordered sleep than their peers without sleep abnormalities.

Obesity. Laboratory research has found that short sleep duration results in metabolic changes that may be linked to obesity.

Depression. The relationship between sleep and depression is complex. While sleep disturbance has long been held to be an important symptom of depression, recent research has indicated that depressive symptoms may decrease once sleep apnea has been effectively treated and sufficient sleep restored. The interrelatedness of sleep and depression suggests it is important that the sleep sufficiency of persons with depression be assessed and that symptoms of depression be monitored among persons with a sleep disorder.

Per the health finder website, http://www.healthfinder. gov/prevention/view:

You need plenty of sleep to stay healthy. Getting a good night's sleep can have many benefits:

1. You will be less likely to get sick.
2. You will be more likely to stay at a healthy weight.
3. You can boost your brainpower and your mood.
4. You can think more clearly and do better in school and at work.
5. You can make better decisions and avoid injuries. For example, sleepy drivers cause thousands of car crashes every year.
6. You can lower your risk of high blood pressure and diabetes.

How much sleep do I need?

Most adults need 7 to 8 hours of sleep each night. If you are having trouble sleeping, make changes to your routine to get the sleep you need. For example, stay away from caffeine in the afternoon.

Kids need even more sleep than adults.

1. Teens need at least 9 hours of sleep each night.
2. School-aged and preschool children need 10 to 12 hours of sleep.
3. Newborns sleep between 16 and 18 hours a day.

To help you get the sleep you need:

1. Exercise earlier in the day, not right before you go to bed.
2. Stay away from drinks and food with caffeine (such as coffee, tea, soda, or chocolate) late in the day.
3. If you have trouble sleeping at night, limit daytime naps to less than 1 hour.
4. If you drink alcohol, drink only in moderation. Alcohol can keep you from sleeping soundly.
5. Don't eat a big meal close to bedtime.

In conclusion, I would like to thank all of the Organizations who granted me permission to use their valuable information found on their websites in my book.